AF256025

Authors's Introduction:

Have you ever had a friend who always makes you feel better? Well, this book is about a friend like that! His name is Faskin, and he's a very special friend who really cares.

Writing about Faskin reminded me of my childhood and all the nice things my friends and I did for each other.

This book is dedicated to Troy, Mia, and Stella.

Faskin is a very special kind of friend.

He's not only great at patching up small scrapes and nursing minor cuts and bruises, he's also good at problem-solving and reminding his friends to stay positive.

WORRY
STRESS
LISTEN
SHARE
TALK
SYMPTOMS
FEELINGS
HELP
SUPPORT

One Sunday afternoon, Stella was busy planning her birthday party.

Stella was a ballerina and liked things to be perfect.

But this meant that everything she did took a very long time.

There were only a few hours left until the start of her party and there was still so much to do! Stella was starting to feel very stressed and worried.

What if she couldn't get it all done in time?

Stella's tummy started to feel strange and her head was buzzing.

"Oh no, oh no!" she said. "I'm running out of time. What am I going to do?"

She decided to call her friend, Faskin, because he was very good at solving problems.

"Faskin, I really need your help. My party is in a few hours' time and I still have loads to do!" She cried.

"Don't worry, Stella! I'm on my way!" Faskin replied.

6
WORRY
STRESS
LISTEN
BULLYING

It didn't take long for Faskin to arrive at Stella's house.

As he entered her bedroom, he saw Stella sitting at her desk looking stressed and fed up.

He noticed a sheet of paper on the desk with the title 'To-do list'.

There were a lot of items on the list and only a few had been crossed off.

Laying on the floor next to the desk was a pile of guest invites that obviously needed to be sent out.

LISTEN
TALK
FEELINGS
SUPPORT
HELP
SHARE
SYMPTOMS
8

"Oh Faskin, there's not enough time to sort out everything! I wanted my party to be perfect, but it's going to be a disaster!" Stella exclaimed.

"Hey Stella, there's still time!" Faskin replied. "We'll do what we can. Try to be more positive. May I see your to-do list?"

Faskin picked up the list and read through it. His eyebrows raised in surprise.

"This is quite a lot, Stella. Do you really think we need to have a huge balloon house, dress a horse up like a unicorn and book a live pop band?"

Stella giggled, "Well, when you say it aloud, it does sound a bit silly," she said. "I was so focussed on the party being perfect, I didn't think about what was possible!"

"No worries!" replied Faskin. "I have a plan. I'll call Isabella and see if she can bake some cakes, and Poppy and Sophia are great at planning parties! Let's ask them for help setting up. While we're waiting for them to get here, I'll take these invites and deliver them to the other guests."

WORRY
LISTEN
CALM
PEER MENTOR
SADNESS
SHARE
TALK
SYMPTOMS
FEELINGS
HELP
SUPPORT

When Poppy and Sophia arrived at Stella's house, they immediately set to work putting up decorations, suggesting fun party games to play and making a music playlist.

They had brought with them the delicious cakes from Isabella.

Stella was over the moon with delight when she saw the cakes.

She picked up the strawberry cake, looked at Sophia and said, "Now that's perfect!"

14

Stella's birthday party was now in full swing and all the guests were laughing and dancing to the music.

No-one seemed to care that there wasn't a huge balloon house, a pretend unicorn or a live pop band.

Everyone was having a great time, including Stella.

When she saw Faskin, she rushed over to give him a hug.

"Thanks, Faskin. I'm so grateful for your help in making my party perfect."

Faskin had a twinkle in his eye as he replied, "Stella, maybe it's perfect because all your friends are here to celebrate your birthday with you."

WORRY
LISTEN
MENTAL
SADNESS
SHARE
TALK
SYMPTOMS
FEELINGS
HELP
SUPPORT

The next day at school, all the talk was about Stella's party.

Stella thought about what Faskin had said last night.

She thought about her friends enjoying themselves and realised Faskin was right, the best part of the party was being with friends.

The following day, Faskin was walking through the park on his way to school. Sitting on a park bench was Miaskye.

She was crying.

Miaskye loved running and animals; she was one of the fastest in her year and was often seen jogging in the park with her dog, Milo.

"Hi Miaskye," Faskin said, sitting down next to her. "What's wrong? You look upset. Do you want to talk about it?"

"It's Milo!" Miaskye sniffed. "He's not feeling well. My mum took him to the vet this morning."

Faskin remembered how worried he had been when his own rabbit, Patch, was sick.

"I'm really sorry to hear that," he said, giving Miaskye a little hug. "Try to think happy thoughts! I bet the vet will help Milo feel better."

Miaskye looked up and nodded her head in agreement.

Just then, her phone rang loudly, making them both jump.

It was her mum with news about Milo. Suddenly, her face lit up.

"Milo's going to be okay! Mum said he only has an upset tummy, so the vet gave him some medicine."

"That's brilliant news!" Faskin replied. "Come on, let's get to school, or we'll be late!"

They both arrived in time before the first lessons started.

Faskin began walking towards the classroom until he noticed another friend, Caspar, looking sad.

Caspar and Faskin were very close friends, ever since the day Faskin saved Caspar from choking on popcorn in the cinema.

Caspar was great at drawing and wanted to be an artist someday.

Entrance

"Hi Caspar, are you alright?" Faskin asked.

"It's just not fair!" Caspar mumbled.

He pointed across the playground. "Tom's being really mean. He keeps teasing me because of the colour of my hair."

Faskin's face got all scrunched up and angry. He felt bad for Caspar.

It just wasn't right to tease someone, especially about something they couldn't change.

Faskin knew he had to do something.

So, he took a deep breath to calm himself and walked over to Tom.

"Hey, Tom! Stop picking on Caspar," Faskin said.

"That's not cool. You wouldn't like it if someone teased you, would you? It's not nice to make people feel bad about themselves."

Tom's eyes widened with surprise; he wasn't used to people standing up to him.

He stopped to think about what Faskin had said.

It was clear he felt embarrassed.

After a moment, he mumbled, "Sorry, Caspar," before walking away.

Caspar was so surprised! "Wow, Faskin! Thanks for sticking up for me!" he said.

"Did you know you're the only one who has ever been brave enough to tell Tom to stop? You're the best friend ever, and a hero too!"

Faskin grinned. "It's important to say something when you see something wrong," he said.

"I hope Tom learns to be nicer. I think he's a good person inside."

Isabella loved baking, especially yummy cakes and cookies! She always said she wanted her own bakery someday.

She decided to enter a baking contest at school, but she was super nervous! What if the judges didn't like her cookies? What if she came in last place? She felt wobbly inside.

So, she asked Faskin to come with her.

Faskin always knew how to help her feel better, especially after he helped her when she accidentally burned her finger while baking.

When the judges announced the winners, Isabella got third place. Faskin saw that Isabella looked disappointed and wanted to cheer her up.

"Those chocolate chip cookies look delicious!" he said. "Can I try one?" He saw Tom nearby and called him over to try one too.

Isabella watched Faskin and Tom munch, munch, munch on her cookies. "Mmm! These are so yummy, Isabella!" Tom said. Then, because he was trying to be kinder to others since Faskin had stood up to him, he added, "You're an amazing baker."

Faskin smiled. "Always believe in yourself. Third place is really good!"

Isabella thought about what Faskin said. Third place really was a great achievement and she had a whole year to practise baking cookies until she could enter the competition again.

It had been a busy week at Highfield Junior School.

When the bell rang for home time, everyone started packing up their things.

Faskin was about to leave with Caspar when he saw Troy, the ace school football player, looking worried.

"Are you okay, Troy?" Faskin asked.

"No," Troy said, "I lost my house key!"

Troy was an awesome football player and was great at scoring goals. One time, Troy scraped his knee during a game. Luckily, Faskin was there to help fix it up! But off the pitch, Troy was always losing things.

"It has to be here somewhere," Faskin said. "I'll help you look for it."

"Me too!" said Caspar, who hadn't noticed Troy looking upset until Faskin spoke to him. They looked everywhere. Finally, Faskin found the key! It was hiding under the mat by the desk.

"Thanks, Faskin," said Troy, relieved. "My dad says I'd lose my head if it wasn't screwed on."

"It's a good thing you don't lose the ball when you're trying to score!" Faskin joked. The boys all laughed and started walking home together.

It was the weekend and Faskin's friends wanted to go and see a movie. They met at the park, but Faskin wasn't there!

"Where's Faskin?" asked Miaskye.

"I don't think he has money for a ticket," Stella said.

"Oh," said Troy, "I saw him give his money to Tom the other day. Tom didn't have any lunch money."

"Wow!" said Isabella. "That was nice."

"Let's do something nice for him!" Caspar said.

"How about a movie night at his house?" Stella suggested.

They all agreed that a movie night was a great idea, so the friends went to Faskin's house.

Faskin was out, helping his dad shop for groceries, so his mum let them in.

Isabella brought cookies, which were even better than the ones she'd made for the competition.

Troy remembered he had lots of fizzy drinks
he could bring.

Miaskye brought popcorn, and carrots for
Patch.

Caspar drew a banner to put over Faskin's
door and Stella arranged fairy lights and
decorations until everything was just right.

When Faskin came home, he was so surprised! He had been sad that he was missing out on seeing a movie with his friends, but now his friends had brought the movie to him!

They all sat together, watching the movie, wrapped up warm in cosy blankets, eating popcorn and drinking fizzy drinks.

After the movie, they talked about Faskin.

"Faskin helped calm me down when I was stressed," Stella said. "He helped make my party perfect!"

"He comforted me when Milo was sick," Miaskye said quietly. "I was so worried and he sat with me and talked me through until we got the good news."

"He stood up for me when Tom was being mean," said Caspar. "No-one's ever done that for me before."

"He made me feel much better about getting third place in the baking contest," Isabella added.

"And he helped me find my key!" said Troy.

"Why are you so kind, Faskin?" Isabella asked.

"And how did you notice that Troy was sad?" Caspar added. "I would have left if you hadn't said something."

"I just pay attention to people," Faskin said. "If they look sad, I ask if I can help."

Faskin thought for a moment, wondering how he could properly explain.

Then he remembered his favourite poem and said it aloud to his friends...

"We should always help a friend in need,

To care for others is a thoughtful deed.

A listening ear and comforting tone

Means someone is never left alone."

Everyone smiled.

They were happy to be friends with Faskin. Not only was he always there to help them with their problems, but he taught them a lot about how they could be special friends themselves.

The End.

Points for Discussion

Let's see what we have learned from the story. Try to answer the questions below:

Q1. What type of friend is Faskin?

Q2. How did Faskin help Miaskye feel better about her dog?

Q3. Why was Caspar upset at school?

Q4. What advice did Faskin give to Stella when she was worried about her party?

Q5. What did Isabella learn about coming third in the baking competition?

Q6. How did Troy find his front door key?

Q7. What did Faskin's friends do when Faskin was sad?

Q8. What is the one thing from the poem you can use to help others?

Q9. How might Faskin have felt if no-one had helped him when he was sad?

Q10. What do you think makes a special friend?

Kingsley Ogedengbe is a dedicated father of three and the author behind engaging children's books that explore the vital skills of first aid and emotional well-being. A qualified First Aid Trainer and Mental Health Trainer, Kingsley also brings his expertise as a Personal Trainer to his work, running training courses that empower both adults and children with essential life skills. Through his books, Kingsley aims to inspire young readers to discover the importance of caring for themselves and each other.

Books Published By Author (Available On Amazon)